TODAY'S
SUPERSTARS

Shaun
White

By Mike Kennedy

Gareth Stevens
Publishing

Please visit our web site at www.garethstevens.com.
For a free catalog describing Gareth Stevens Publishing's list of high-quality books,
call 1-800-542-2595 (USA) or 1-800-387-3178 (Canada).
Gareth Stevens Publishing's fax: 1-877-542-2596

Library of Congress Cataloging-in-Publication Data
Kennedy, Mike (Mike William), 1965–
        Shaun White / by Mike Kennedy.
          p. cm. — (Today's superstars)
        Includes bibliographical references and index.
        ISBN-10: 1-4339-1968-0   ISBN-13: 978-1-4339-1968-8 (lib. bdg.)
        ISBN-10: 1-4339-2161-8   ISBN-13: 978-1-4339-2161-2 (soft cover)
        1. White, Shaun, 1986– —Juvenile literature. 2. Snowboarders—United States—
    Biography—Juvenile literature. I. Title.
    GV857.S57W555   2010
    796.22092—dc22   2009007172

This edition first published in 2010 by
Gareth Stevens Publishing
A Weekly Reader® Company
1 Reader's Digest Road
Pleasantville, NY 10570-7000 USA

Copyright © 2010 by Gareth Stevens, Inc.

Executive Managing Editor: Lisa M. Herrington
Senior Designer: Keith Plechaty

Produced by Editorial Directions, Inc.

Art Direction and Page Production: The Design Lab

Photo Credits: cover, title page Steve Dykes/NewSport/Corbis; p. 4 Olivier Maire/epa/Corbis; p. 6 AP
Photo/Richard Drew; p. 7 Olivier Maire/epa/Corbis; p. 8 Frank Micelotta/Getty Images; p. 9 Bo Bridges/
Corbis; p. 10 Bo Bridges/Corbis; p. 13 Mike Powell/Getty Images; p. 14 Eric Gaillard/Reuters/Corbis; p.
15 K.C. Alfred/SDU-T/ZUMA/Corbis; p. 16 AP Photo/Garry Jones; p. 18 Tim Rue/Corbis; p. 19, 41 AP
Photo/Keystone, Arno Balzarini; p. 20, 46 Tim Rue/Corbis; p. 21 AP Photo/Douglas C. Pizac; p. 22 Jed
Jacobsohn/Getty Images; p. 24 Chris Polk/WireImage; p. 25 KMazur/WireImage for ESPN; p. 26, 40 K.C.
Alfred/SDU-T/ZUMA/Corbis; p. 27 AP Photo/Jeff Christensen; p. 28 AP Photo/Jeff Christensen; p. 30 AP
Photo/Matt Sayles; p. 31 Mike Ehrmann/Getty Images; p. 32 AP Photo/Mark Duncan; p. 33 AP Photo/
Mark J. Terrill; p. 34 Franco Debernardi/epa/Corbis; p. 36 Justin Kase Conder-US Presswire; p. 37 John
Shearer/WireImage; p. 38 James Devaney/WireImage; p. 39 Soren McCarty/WireImage

Printed in the United States of America

1 2 3 4 5 6 7 8 9 14 13 12 11 10 09

Contents

Words in the glossary appear in **bold** type the first time they are used in the text.

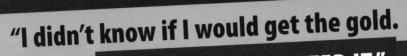

"I didn't know if I would get the gold. I JUST KNEW I WANTED IT."

—Shaun White

Shaun White flies above the halfpipe at the 2006 Winter Olympics in Italy.

2006

Chapter 1
Good as Gold

Shaun White knew what he had to do. He had dreamed of winning an Olympic gold medal in snowboarding since he was a boy. Now he was at the 2006 Winter Olympics in Torino, Italy. He was in the final of the men's **halfpipe** competition. At this moment, he had a chance to make his lifelong dream come true. White took in the scene around him and could barely contain his excitement.

A huge crowd had gathered to watch White and his fellow riders. Fans from all over the world filled the stands. They waved the flags of their countries proudly. They shouted out encouragement for their favorite snowboarders. The people in the crowd were as excited as White was.

All About Shaun

Name: Shaun Roger White

Birth Date: September 3, 1986

Birthplace: Carlsbad, California

Height: 5 feet 9 inches (175 centimeters)

Weight: 145 pounds (66 kilograms)

Home Mountain: Park City Mountain Resort (Utah)

Family: Parents, Kathy and Roger; sister, Kerri; brother, Jesse

Fact File

White was named after his dad's favorite pro surfer, Shaun Thompson.

Tough Start

No one doubted that White was the best snowboarder on the planet. Fans called him the Flying Tomato for his amazing **aerial** tricks and his long, flowing red hair. However, he had not been at his best early in the competition.

White, in fact, had almost failed to make the halfpipe final. In qualifying, he botched his landing on his first run, putting him in seventh place. Only the top six would compete in the finals. But White met the challenge. On his second run, he responded with a great performance. He scored high enough to reach the finals.

Full Tilt on the Halfpipe

White felt confident as he sped down the halfpipe for his first run in the final. The crowd cheered loudly. The fans sensed that something special was about to happen. They were right.

White was magnificent. He nailed every jump he attempted. At one point, he landed back-to-back 1080s. The judges were impressed. White earned a score of 46.8 points out of a possible 50.

TRUE OR FALSE?

White has a dog named Bozo.

For answers, see page 46.

Three's a Charm

A 1080 is a very difficult trick—and one of White's **signature** jumps. It requires the rider to do three full turns in the air and then land safely on the ground. Few riders can match White when it comes to doing a 1080. What does he really think of the jump? "1080s are cool, but they're not fun to do," he says.

▶ White grabs his board as he performs a 1080.

Tears of Joy

When White saw his score, he raised his arms in the air and shouted in celebration. It would be nearly impossible for anyone to beat him. He had just pulled off the greatest performance of his life. "I didn't know if I would get the gold. I just knew I wanted it," White said later.

One by one, the rest of the snowboarders made their runs. No one could equal White's grace or **precision**. The gold medal was his. At the medal ceremony, he flashed a big smile, and a few tears ran down his face.

TRUE OR FALSE?

White has won an Olympic gold medal as a skateboarder.

Fame Game

White is one of the most famous extreme athletes in the world. After the 2006 Winter Olympics, for example, he got a big hug from Tom Cruise. White, however, prefers a more low-key lifestyle. "Through snowboarding I have been lucky enough to meet a lot of celebrities," he says. "It's cool because they are always fun and have great stories. In the end, I have the most fun just hanging out with my close friends riding or chilling out."

▶ **White hangs out with Lil Jon (center) and Pharrell Williams at the 2006 MTV Video Music Awards.**

Flying High

White's gold medal at the 2006 Winter Olympics fulfilled one of his childhood dreams. There are many more he wants to achieve. He has also carved out an incredible career as a skateboarder. He helped create a best-selling video game, and he has his own line of snowboard apparel and equipment.

▲ White is as talented on a skateboard as he is on a snowboard.

White, however, isn't motivated by fame and money. He loves the freedom and creativity of snowboarding and skateboarding. To him, nothing is more thrilling than feeling the wind whip through his hair as he soars through the air. For White, the sky isn't the limit. It's where dreams become reality.

Fact File

In addition to the Flying Tomato, other nicknames for White are Future Boy, Señor Blanco, and the Egg.

> # "I could always just set my mind to it, see THE TRICK IN MY MIND AND THEN DO IT."
> —Shaun White

White has loads of natural ability. But he credits his family with helping him achieve success.

Chapter 2

Heart of a Champion

Some athletes are "naturals." Their talent is obvious the first time they try a sport. That is one way to describe Shaun White. He started snowboarding at age six. From there, it was only a short step to skateboarding. For him, it was a fun sport to do in the summer. "I could always just set my mind to it, see the trick in my mind and then do it."

That doesn't mean White's road to stardom was easy. He suffered from serious heart problems as a child. Since then, he has relied on his loving family—and his love of snowboarding and skateboarding—to overcome every challenge he has faced.

Health Matters

Shaun Roger White was born on September 3, 1986, in Carlsbad, California. He was the last of three children. His parents, Roger and Kathy, worked hard to support Shaun, his brother, Jesse, and sister, Kerri. They taught their kids to be kind and curious.

The family got a scare when Shaun was a baby. Doctors diagnosed a problem with Shaun's heart. As blood pumped through his body, it did not carry the proper amount of oxygen. Shaun needed to have surgery on his heart. Doctors performed two operations to correct the problem.

Fact File

Shaun, Jesse, and Kerri nicknamed their dad Homer after *The Simpsons* character.

12

Fast and Furious

Everyone in the White family was a good athlete. In fact, both of Shaun's grandparents on his mother's side were **roller derby** stars. In the summer, the Whites hit the beach and went surfing. In the winter, they drove to the mountains of California for ski trips.

Shaun had no fear on the slopes. Roger and Kathy worried every time they watched him barrel down a mountain on his skis. When Shaun turned six, his parents suggested he try snowboarding. To slow him down, they taught him to ride backward. They hoped Shaun would be less of a danger that way.

TRUE OR FALSE?

Shaun's favorite sport to watch is motocross.

Brotherly Love

Shaun learned to snowboard by watching his brother. Jesse, who is six years older, is also a good snowboarder. After Shaun's first day of snowboarding, he was doing virtually everything that his big brother could do. To this day, Jesse is Shaun's favorite snowboarding buddy. "We push each other in different ways, but it's always about progression and making each other better," White says.

▲ Shaun and Jesse (right) are not only brothers, but good friends.

A Real Competitor

After just one year on a snowboard, Shaun was ready for competition. He entered his first meet in 1993 and won it. He later earned a spot in the national snowboarding championships for children 12 years old and younger. He finished in 11th place.

Shaun caught everyone's attention with his high-flying snowboarding style. He rose far above the halfpipe and landed tricks that others his age could not do. He was also a fierce competitor. No one wanted to win more than he did.

TRUE OR FALSE?

Shaun White is the only halfpipe champion in his family.

Bandanna Man

Shaun White always wears a bandanna when he snowboards. He started doing this by accident. As a kid, he got sunburned easily. To protect his skin, he wore a ski mask or used sunscreen. One day on the slopes, he lent his sunscreen to a friend. She forgot to give it back. White didn't have a mask with him, so he grabbed a T-shirt and wrapped it across his face. It worked perfectly. The next day, White switched to a bandanna. He has used one ever since.

▲ White wore a red, white, and blue bandanna at the 2006 Olympics.

Keep On Truckin'

Shaun's success was good news to his family. The Whites began making more and more trips to snowboarding competitions. They traveled all over the western states. Everyone had fun on these mini-vacations.

The Whites were not wealthy, so they found a unique way to get where they were going. The family would pile into an old van that they called Big Mo. Sometimes they slept in the van to save money on hotels. When the Whites pulled into a resort, everyone knew that Shaun had arrived.

▲ Shaun shares his success with his parents. Here, they pose with Shaun's Olympic gold medal.

Fact File

White learned his remarkable midair body control on the family's backyard trampoline.

"I've got to win, that's all I cared about, **EVEN WHEN I WAS YOUNGER.**"

—Shaun White

White speeds down the halfpipe on his skateboard. He practices hard because he loves to win.

Chapter 3
Future Boy

What makes a world-class snowboarder or skateboarder? Talent is important, but it takes more than that. The best riders practice all the time. They are constantly searching for ways to improve.

Shaun White learned this lesson when he was very young. His parents taught him the value of hard work. With his brother and sister, he learned the importance of friendly competition. Shaun especially loved to compete against Jesse. Anything that his older brother did, Shaun wanted to do better.

"I've got to win, that's all I cared about, even when I was younger," he has said. This competitive spirit helped him become a star in two sports.

Getting Noticed

For the Whites, Mount Hood in Oregon became their home away from home. They made friends with an instructor named Tim Windell. He ran a skiing and snowboarding camp. Seeing Shaun's talent, he offered the Whites a discount on Shaun's lessons.

TRUE OR FALSE?

When Shaun was a kid, he was a big fan of *Pokemon*.

Windell wasn't the only one impressed by Shaun. In 1995, skateboarding legend Tony Hawk spotted him on the slopes. He raved about Shaun to others in the extreme sports world. Shaun became known as Future Boy. Everyone expected him to become a star.

The Bird Man

All extreme athletes have one person to thank for their success: Tony Hawk. Known as the Bird Man, Hawk is the greatest skateboarder ever. He has invented more tricks and won more titles than anyone else in the sport. His popularity paved the way for all other extreme sports, including snowboarding. White has a special relationship with Hawk. "He's grown into his own style," says Hawk of White, "plus he can do tricks five feet higher than everyone else does them."

▶ **Skateboarding star Tony Hawk (right) knew young Shaun was destined to be a star.**

Going Pro

The more training Shaun received, the better he got. He did everything on his snowboard. He competed in halfpipe events and races. Not surprisingly, he won just about every competition he entered.

After his 13th birthday, Shaun turned pro. This meant he would be paid to be a snowboarder. If he won an event, he would collect a paycheck. Companies would also be able to **sponsor** him to use their products. This was another way to earn money as an athlete.

▲ As Shaun won more events, he decided to turn pro. This way, he could make a living as an extreme athlete.

Fact File

In the movie *Happy Gilmore*, rebel golfer Happy wins a series of giant checks. The movie made White want to win a giant check of his own.

New Kid on the Block

Shaun White's decision to go pro provided a big boost for snowboarding. Back in the 1990s, many people weren't sure what to think about snowboarders. Were they "real athletes" or just **daredevils** who liked the thrill of speeding down a mountain or catching air on the halfpipe?

When sports fans watched White, they saw a real athlete. On the halfpipe, he was graceful and focused. He was also a good kid who came from a good family. People began to look at snowboarding in a more positive light.

Fact File

In 1996, White won three of the four events at the national junior championships.

Serious About Skating

White has been skateboarding almost as long as he's been snowboarding. In 2000, he decided to get more serious about his skateboarding career. He has learned a lot about the sport since then, but he admits that skateboarding will always be more difficult than snowboarding. "I'm used to doing airs and stuff in snowboarding," he says. "I think it's so much harder to go big and do the tricks [in skateboarding]. They're so much faster and so much less under control."

Agony of Defeat

White worked hard to be taken seriously on snowboarding's pro tour. Many of his competitors thought of him as a cute little brother. That started to change in 2000. White finished second in several events and competed in the X Games for the first time.

In 2001, White wowed the judges during a halfpipe competition in Salt Lake City, Utah. With the next Olympics only a year away, he imagined the rush of winning a gold medal. But he didn't qualify for the 2002 Winter Games. He missed making the U.S. team by 0.3 points. He was crushed, and he vowed to pick up his game.

▲ White does a trick on the halfpipe during the 2001 World Cup.

TRUE OR FALSE?

Snowboarding became an Olympic sport in 1998.

"When the pressure's on, I always seem to go **BIGGER AND LAND EVERYTHING BETTER.**"

—Shaun White

White is at his best when the pressure is high.

Chapter 4

X-cited

Pressure affects different people in different ways. Athletes who perform well when the competition is at its toughest are known as being clutch. Under extreme pressure, they concentrate harder and raise their performance. "When the pressure's on, I always seem to go bigger and land everything better," White says.

Without a doubt, White falls into the category of clutch performers. After he missed out on the 2002 Olympics, people wondered how he would respond. The pressure was on to perform. White never backed down. Instead, he took the challenge and rode with it. He became more determined than ever to make his mark in snowboarding and skateboarding.

First and Foremost

White opened 2003 at the Winter X Games. The rest of the snowboarders in the competition didn't know what hit them. White took the gold medal in the halfpipe and **slopestyle** events.

That was just the beginning of an incredible year for White. He finished first in eight more events, including the slopestyle at the U.S. Open. He also took his skateboarding career to the next level. In August, he competed in the Summer X Games for the first time.

Fact File

White was named Action Sports Athlete of the Year at the 2003 ESPY Awards.

Extreme Competition

The X Games are similar to the Olympics except they are for extreme athletes. The competition started in 1995 and takes place twice a year, in the winter and the summer. Sports in the Winter X Games include skiing, snowboarding, and snowmobiling. Sports in the Summer X Games include adventure racing, surfing, skateboarding, and BMX. Athletes from all over the world compete in the X Games. They are broadcast on television by ESPN.

◀ **White catches serious air during the 2003 Summer X Games.**

Crossing Over

White's success in 2003 had a huge impact on his life. No athlete before him had become a star in snowboarding and skateboarding. By crossing over between the two sports, he was making history.

He was also making a lot of money and a lot of headlines. The list of companies that wanted to sponsor him continued to grow. Writers and reporters seemed to call every day asking for interviews. Being a celebrity was a new challenge for White. He enjoyed the attention but didn't allow it to distract him.

▲ White doesn't let fame distract him. Here he appears with Billy Bush on the red carpet at the 2004 ESPY Awards.

TRUE OR FALSE?

Shaun White was the first athlete to compete in both the Winter X Games and Summer X Games.

▲ White celebrates after winning the gold medal in the slopestyle at the 2004 Winter X Games.

Fact File

Shaun White's sponsors include Target, Burton Snowboards, and Birdhouse Skateboards.

Recovery Plan

White was ready for another big year in 2004. He started well by winning the gold medal in the slopestyle at the Winter X Games. He then finished first in three more competitions.

White was feeling great—until he suffered a serious knee injury. The pain was intense. He had been hurt before, however, and each time he had returned to full health. This time was no different. After six months of **rehabilitation**, White was back on his snowboard.

Getting Fit

White's knee injury was a turning point for him. He realized how much he loved snowboarding and skateboarding. The thought of not being able to compete in either sport scared him. That motivated him to get stronger.

White decided to get in better shape and take better care of himself. The 2006 Winter Olympics were less than two years away. He wasn't going to take any chances. He wanted to win Olympic gold.

Sounds Good

In 2004, White released a DVD called *The Shaun White Album*. The video tells the story of his life and shows footage of some of his tricks. For many fans, one of the best parts of the DVD is the soundtrack. White helped pick the songs. They include "Showdown" by Electric Light Orchestra, "Crazy On You" by Heart, "Mad World" by Tears for Fears, "Black Betty" by Ram Jam, "Juke Box Hero" by Foreigner, and "Blinded by the Light" by Manfred Mann's Earth Band.

▶ When White isn't on a snowboard or a skateboard, he enjoys music.

"It's nice to be able to speak my mind."

—Shaun White

White holds his gold medal backstage during MTV's *Total Request Live.*

Chapter 5

The Flying Tomato

Is being famous all it's cracked up to be? It depends on the person. Some people like reading about themselves in magazines and seeing themselves on television. Others prefer their privacy. They don't like being in the spotlight.

White has discovered that fame can be a lot of fun. He has also found out that it can help him achieve his goals. Fame gives him a chance to reach out to his fans. He gets to talk about things that are important to him. "It's nice to be able to speak my mind," he says. Being famous also helped him turn snowboarding into one of the world's most popular extreme sports.

Back on Top

White returned to full health in 2005. He showed it with a gold in the slopestyle at the Winter X Games. He followed that with first-place finishes in seven other events.

White also made important strides as a skateboarder. He earned the first championship of his career, in the **vert** at the Panasonic Open in Louisville, Kentucky. At the Summer X Games, he won the silver medal in the vert.

TRUE OR FALSE?

White snowboarded down dangerous mountains in Alaska for a 2005 movie.

The Dating Game

Heading into the 2006 Winter Olympics, White joked that he had a crush U.S. figure skater Sasha Cohen. The media thought he was serious. The pair seemed like a perfect match. For the next few weeks, White's love life was all that some reporters talked about. The attention was embarrassing for him. His joke didn't seem that funny anymore. On the bright side, he got to meet Cohen a few months later. "She's cool," he said.

◀ Reporters thought Sasha Cohen was the perfect match for White.

Star Power

White was the talk of the snowboarding world. In January 2006, he scored his second Winter X Games double when he won the halfpipe and slopestyle. With the Winter Olympics only weeks away, everyone expected him to take the gold in the men's halfpipe in Italy.

Meanwhile, White's fame grew. He appeared on magazine covers and did television interviews. The media loved his story. He was young and cool. His nickname, the Flying Tomato, was unusual. And White wasn't afraid to give his opinion when asked a question.

▲ By 2006, White was used to being mobbed by fans almost everywhere he went.

Fact File

In 2006, White was named Rider of the Year by *Transworld Snowboarding* and *Transworld Skateboarding*.

Olympic Glory

The 2006 Winter Olympics proved to be one of the best moments of White's life. He was a little nervous when the snowboarding competition began. That was clear during his qualifying runs. White struggled to make the final of the men's halfpipe.

He found his rhythm in his first run in the final. He landed all six of his jumps. At one point, he did back-to-back 1080s. His performance was almost perfect. He won the gold medal easily.

TRUE OR FALSE?

White has landed 1080s in skateboarding and snowboarding.

▼ White celebrates his gold medal win with teammate and silver medal–winner Danny Kass.

32

Car Toy

Winning a gold medal is an incredible achievement. White knows this as well as anyone. He also understands how to keep such an accomplishment in perspective. In an interview after the 2006 Winter Olympics, he was asked about the best way to show off his gold medal. He thought for a moment and joked, "I could hang it from the rearview mirror of my car."

▲ White shows his gold medal to talk show host Jay Leno.

Coming Home

White was amazed by the way he was treated after the Olympics. He became a hero to thousands of kids across the United States. Talk-show hosts lined up to get him on their programs. Dozens of new companies wanted to sponsor him.

White didn't want all the attention to go to his head. He relied on his family to help him stay grounded. He also remembered what he enjoyed most about snowboarding. The fame and celebrity were fun, but nothing was better than catching air on the halfpipe.

Fact File

White appeared on the cover of *Sports Illustrated* after the 2006 Winter Olympics.

"I just want people to see me as an all-around RIDER WHO CAN DO ANYTHING."

—Shaun White

White's Olympic win made him eager to take the next step in his career.

Chapter 6

A Wild Ride

Extreme athletes look at the world differently from most other people. They are always pushing the limits of what they can do. What many people view as obstacles, extreme athletes see as exciting new challenges. "I just want people to see me as an all-around rider who can do anything," White says.

After White's gold medal win at the 2006 Winter Olympics, he couldn't wait to take the next step in his career. He never looks back or takes it easy. Each day is an opportunity to try something new. For him, life has always been a wild ride, and he looks forward to every thrilling up and down.

Open Champ

What was next for White? He had won just about every snowboard competition there was — except the overall championship at the U.S. Open. Though he had won the slopestyle event at this competition, he had yet to win the halfpipe. He needed to win both to be the overall champion. This title meant a lot to him. The event was sponsored by Burton. He worked with this company to design snowboarding equipment.

Finally, in 2006, White got the title he wanted. He took both the halfpipe and slopestyle events, making him the overall champion. The following year, he made history again. Burton launched a new snowboarding series known as the Global Open. White claimed the crown. He was just as proud that August when he won skateboarding gold in the vert at the Summer X Games.

▲ White soars above a rail during a slopestyle event in 2006.

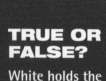

TRUE OR FALSE?

White holds the record for most Winter X Games medals.

Onward and Upward

White continued to explore new interests in 2008. He served as the **guest editor** for an issue of *Snowboarder* magazine. He also launched a video game called *Shaun White Snowboarding*. It was an instant hit with snowboarders and gaming fans.

On the slopes, White won the halfpipe at the U.S. Open for the third year in a row. He captured the gold at the Winter X Games in the superpipe (which had been known as the halfpipe). In the new Winter Dew Tour, he earned a gold in the slopestyle and a silver in the superpipe.

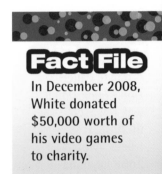

Fact File

In December 2008, White donated $50,000 worth of his video games to charity.

Game Time

The *Shaun White Snowboarding* video game is available for all game systems. It took two years to develop. And White was involved in creating it. His voice is used in the game, and he also helped re-create his jumps. He wore a **motion-capture** suit that recorded his movements exactly. He didn't actually get on a snowboard. Instead, he used a skateboard, which worked much better with the motion-capture technology.

▶ White shows students how to play his video game on the *Wii Fit*.

Double Threat

White added another extraordinary chapter to his career at the 2009 Winter X Games. He won the slopestyle without much trouble. He was the only rider in the competition to "cross the channel," which was the course's most difficult jump.

A day later, it looked as if White would miss out on the gold in the superpipe. He fell on his first two runs. He needed the run of his life on his third attempt to pass leader Kevin Pearce. White was up for the challenge. He beat Pearce by one point and claimed a record-setting ninth gold medal at the Winter X Games.

Fact File

A movie called *Don't Look Down* was released in 2008. It tracks White's 2006 Olympic experience.

His Favorite Mountain

White has snowboarded all over the globe. Does he have a favorite resort or mountain? It's hard for him to decide. "There are a couple places that are always fun," he says. "The Park City park is awesome. Riding in Colorado and Tahoe is always a blast. Japan is just fun to visit and experience. Overall, I try to have a blast wherever I am."

◄ White doesn't care as much about where he snowboards as he does about having a good time.

R.E.D. BURT

Risk and Reward

Snowboarding and skateboarding have taught White a lot about life. So have his parents, brother, and sister. To him, nothing is impossible.

White brings this attitude to everything he does. It might be writing music for a new song. It might be donating his time and money to a charity. It might be teaching kids how to land a jump on the superpipe. If White can dream it, he can do it.

"The greatest lesson I have learned is to trust myself and believe in the decisions that I make," White says. "You have to have confidence in yourself in order to take the risky route and come out on top."

By the Numbers

6 The age at which White snowboarded for the first time

12 The number of snowboarding events White won in a row from 2005 to 2006

14 The number of Winter X Games medals White had after the 2009 competition

46.8 The score that won White the halfpipe gold medal at the 2006 Winter Olympics

1080 The jump that White has made famous

Time Line

1986 Shaun White is born on September 3 in Carlsbad, California.

1992 White gets on a snowboard for the first time.

1993 White wins his first snowboarding competition.

1999 White turns pro in snowboarding.

2003 White wins the halfpipe and slopestyle at the Winter X Games.

2005 White wins his first skateboarding title.

2006 White wins the halfpipe gold at the Winter Olympics.

2007 White wins the vert gold at the Summer X Games.

2008 *Shaun White Snowboarding* is released.

2009 White sets a record with his ninth Winter X Games gold medal.

Glossary

aerial: something that happens in the air

daredevils: people who get a thrill from doing things that are dangerous

guest editor: a temporary job at a magazine. A guest editor helps produce a specific issue.

halfpipe: an event at snowboarding competitions; a snowboarding ramp that looks like a round pipe cut into a semicircle

motion-capture: relating to the process of recording the movements of a person and then translating them digitally for animation

precision: exactness or accuracy

rehabilitation: the process of recovering from an injury

roller derby: a sport in which teams roller-skate around an oval rink

signature: a quality or thing that sets someone apart from others

slopestyle: a snowboarding competition in which riders complete tricks on rails and jumps

sponsor: to pay an athlete to train and compete in return for that athlete promoting a company's product

vert: a skateboarding event in which riders do tricks on a larger version of a halfpipe

To Find Out More

Books

Fitzpatrick, Jim. *Snowboarding* (21st Century Skills Innovation Library). Ann Arbor, MI: Cherry Lake Publishing, 2008.

Kennedy, Mike. *Tony Hawk* (People We Should Know). Pleasantville, NY: Gareth Stevens Publishing, 2010.

Stewart, Mark. *Olympics* (The Ultimate 10). Pleasantville, NY: Gareth Stevens Publishing, 2008.

Web Sites

JockBio.com: Shaun White
www.jockbio.com/Bios/Swhite/Swhite_bio.html
Find out biographical information, facts, and what others say about White.

Shaun White
www.shaunwhite.com
Get the latest information on White's career in snowboarding and skateboarding.

Shaun White Snowboarding
shaunwhitegame.us.ubi.com
Get a full overview of Shaun's video game.

Championships

Winter Olympics
| Gold | 2006 | Men's Halfpipe |

Winter X Games
Silver	2002	Slopestyle
Silver	2002	Halfpipe
Gold	2003	Slopestyle
Gold	2003	Halfpipe
Gold	2004	Slopestyle
Gold	2005	Slopestyle
Gold	2006	Slopestyle
Gold	2006	Halfpipe
Silver	2007	Superpipe
Bronze	2007	Slopestyle
Bronze	2008	Slopestyle
Gold	2008	Superpipe
Gold	2009	Slopestyle
Gold	2009	Superpipe

Summer X Games
Silver	2005	Vert
Gold	2007	Vert
Bronze	2008	Vert

Source Notes

p. 7 Gavin Edwards, "Shaun White: Attack of the Flying Tomato," *Rolling Stone*, February 24, 2006.

p. 8 (top) Red Bull interview, ShaunWhite.com, 2009.

p. 8 (bottom) "Shaun White Storms to Victory in Olympic Half-Pipe," *World Snowboard Guide*, February 12, 2006, http://worldsnowboardguide.com/news/story/20060212white.cfm.

p. 11 "Adrenaline Rush: Shaun White," *AnOtherMan*, Spring/Summer 2007.

p. 13 Red Bull interview.

p. 17 "Adrenaline Rush: Shaun White."

p. 18 Edwards, *Rolling Stone*.

p. 20 Steve Cave, "Shaun White Profile," About.com: Skateboarding, 2009, http://skateboard.about.com/od/proskaterbios/p/ProShaunWhite.htm.

p. 23 Edwards, *Rolling Stone*.

p. 29 "The White Stuff," *The Red Bulletin*, January 15, 2009, http://uk.redbulletin.com/articles/the_white_stuff/.

p. 30 Ken Lee, "Shaun White Meets Sasha Cohen—At Last," *People*, March 1, 2006, www.people.com/people/article/0,,1168696,00.html.

p. 33 Edwards, *Rolling Stone*.

p. 35 Pat Bridges, "Revived: Shaun White Interview," *Snowboarder*, www.snowboardermag.com/magazine/features/shaun-white-extra/.

p. 38 "Shaun White No. 5 of the 20 Most Influential Riders," *Snowboarder*, www.snowboardermag.com/features/riderprofiles/shaun-white-07/.

p. 39 "Shaun White No. 5."

True or False Answers

Page 7 False. His dog's name is Rambo.

Page 8 False. Skateboarding has yet to be included in the Olympics.

Page 13 True.

Page 14 False. Kerri was the U.S. Open junior champion in 2000.

Page 18 True.

Page 21 True.

Page 25 True.

Page 27 True.

Page 30 True. He starred in the 2005 film *First Descent* with snowboarding legends Hannah Teter, Shawn Farmer, Nick Peralta, and Terje Haakonsen.

Page 32 False. He has attempted the 1080 in skateboarding, but as of 2009, has not landed it.

Page 36 True.

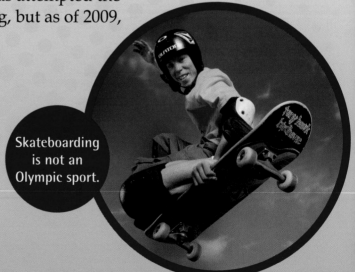

Skateboarding is not an Olympic sport.

Index

About the Author

Mike Kennedy is a huge sports fan who has written dozens of books for kids. He has covered everything from the Super Bowl to skateboarding. Mike grew up in Ridgewood, New Jersey, and went to Franklin & Marshall College, where he earned letters in baseball and football. Today, Mike loves to run on trails and play golf. He and his wife, Ali, live in Boulder, Colorado.